I BELIEVE IN THE HEREAFTER

PILLARS OF FAITH

I BELIEVE IN THE HEREAFTER

Osman Oral

TUGHRA
BOOKS

New Jersey

Copyright © 2014 by Tughra Books

17 16 15 14   1 2 3 4

Published by Tughra Books
345 Clifton Ave., Clifton,
NJ, 07011, USA

www.tughrabooks.com

Library of Congress Cataloging-in-Publication Data Available

ISBN: 978-1-59784-306-5

Printed by
İmak Ofset
Ser. No : 12531
Merkez Mh. Atatürk Cd.
Göl Sk. No: 1 Yenibosna - İSTANBUL
Tel : 0212 656 49 97

Contents

LIFE IN THE GRAVE

THE RIGHTS OF OTHERS

THE RESURRECTION AND
THE DAY OF JUDGMENT

Contents

HEAVEN AND HELL

THE GENEROUS IN HEAVEN

INTERCESSION

Introduction

Believing in Resurrection and the eternal life after death is one of the six pillars of the Islamic faith. According to the Islamic belief, life after death is the true life. As Prophet Muhammad, peace and blessings be upon him, said, "O Allah! There is no true life but the life of the Hereafter, there is no true bliss but the eternal bliss."

The objective in this world is the eternal life after death, therefore denial of the eternal life means perceiving the world as having no true purpose. Human life has no true meaning without a resurrection. We need to always keep in mind the fact that we, as human beings, are created not only for a short worldly life but for eternity, and that on the Day of Judgment our Lord will hold us accountable for the deeds we have committed in this world. Without the Resurrection and the following Divine judgment, neither good nor evil would receive the just and full recompense due to them in this transient world. For this reason, belief in the Hereafter is not only a pillar of faith but also one of the most basic foundations of morality and a sound social life. Indeed, aspiration of the Hereafter conveys a sense of order and harmony in our lives because this world is a field where we sow the seeds of prosperity for an eternal life of bliss.

Relieving us from the terror of disappearing into nothingness after death, our Lord revealed all the previous communities through their Messengers that there will be a resurrection and an everlasting afterlife for both the people of Paradise and the people of the Fire. Every community was cautioned that there will be a judgment following the Resurrection and that the believers' righteous deeds will certainly be rewarded with the eternal life of Paradise, and there will most certainly be punishment for evil. In the last holy Book sent to humankind, Allah the Almighty reveals, again for a last time and in detail, the reason for our creation, our purpose in this life, and the true life which follows death.

This book, titled *I Believe in the Hereafter*, is a compilation of the verses of the Qur'an, the *qudsi hadith*s, or the Divine sayings (narrated by Allah's Messenger but not included in the Qur'an), the sayings of the Messenger of Allah, as well as the reports and wise words of the Companions and other saintly believers, all referring to life in the Hereafter. This work has been written with the sincere aspiration of portraying an accurate account of the life that begins after death, the life of eternity.

I believe in Allah, His angels, His Books, His Prophets, the Hereafter, and the Divine Destiny—that both good and evil take place through the knowledge, law, and creation of Allah the Almighty. I believe that Resurrection in the Hereafter is the truth. I bear witness that there is no deity other than Allah and that Muhammad is the servant and Messenger of Allah.

Belief in the Hereafter

They Awaken with Death

T he Messenger of Allah, peace and blessings be upon him, said, "Be in this world as if you were a stranger or traveler; humans are asleep and they awaken with death."[1/2]

---

[1] Bukhari, Riqaq, 3; al-Ajluni, *Qashfu'l-Khafa*, Vol. 2, p. 414.

[2] No wonder that our beloved Prophet likened us to travelers and our life of this transient world to sleep. Each and every one of us should, indeed, see ourselves as a stranger or traveler in this guesthouse of the world, passing through the stations of our mother's womb, childhood, youth, old age and the grave, and from there, we will go to a completely new world – the eternal life of the Hereafter.

From the perspective of the truths of faith and the truths concerning creation and life, our worldly life is like a dream. So, when human beings die, they awake in the true sense of the word, and their sight and perception becomes much sharper:

"Indeed you were in heedlessness of this (coming before the Supreme Court for judgment), and now We have removed from you your veil, so your sight today is sharp." (Qaf 50:22)

Therefore, all humans, believers and unbelievers alike, will come to understand the truth after their death. What would, however, that understanding avail them if they had not believed and forwarded some good, righteous deeds for their eternal life to come? In this sense, the denial of life after death means perceiving our temporary existence in this world as having no true purpose. We should, however, keep in mind the fact that life does not end at death and that the life of this world is not only transient but consists also of play and pastime in respect to human carnal life.

Abu Lahab and the Flames of Hell

The Messenger of Allah, who was born into the Banu Hashim branch of the Quraysh tribe, climbed the Safa hillock near the Ka'ba in order to convey his message openly to the people of the Quraysh after he received the following Revelations:

The wealth, posts and positions, and social status, to which people tend to attach much importance and on which they depend, are not lasting. Created for lofty purposes, the world is very significant in respect to its being the tillage for the Hereafter. The building-blocks to make up one's Paradise or Hell in the Hereafter are the seeds of one's belief or unbelief and the deeds that one sows here:

"The life of this world is but a (passing) enjoyment, while the Hereafter is indeed the home of permanence. Whoever does an evil is not recompensed except with the like of it; whereas whoever does good, righteous deeds– whether man or woman–and is a believer, such will enter Paradise, being provided there without measure." (Al-Mu'min 40:39–40)

"Say (O Messenger): 'The enjoyment of the world is short-lived, whereas the Hereafter is the best for him who keeps from disobedience to Allah in piety and reverence for Him, and you will not be wronged by so much as a tiny hair.' Wherever you may be, death will find you, even though you be in towers built up strong and high..." (An-Nisa' 4:77– 78; see also Ünal, *The Qur'an with Annotated Interpretation*, 2008, pp. 285, 912)

Therefore, no one will be saved from dying in this world, and no one will stay in the grave eternally. Allah will raise all of the dead, gathering them together in His Presence. He will then hold His servants—who have willpower and who are therefore responsible for their deeds—accountable for the deeds they have committed in this world, and the truth in which they believed or rejected while in the world will become manifest in the Hereafter. This second life is eternal, either in bliss or despair. (Ed.)

And (O Messenger) warn your nearest kinsfolk! Spread your wings (to provide care and shelter) over the believers who follow you (in practicing Allah's commandments in their lives). But if they disobey you (your kinsfolk, by refusing your call; or those who have newly believed, by not giving up their former way of life) then say (to them) "I am free of (responsibility for) what you do." (Ash-Shu'ara 26:214–216)

So from now on, proclaim what you are commanded to convey openly! (Al-Hijr 15:99)

Basing his main message on the Oneness of God and eternal life after death, the Prophet called out, "O the people of Quraysh! Come and gather around, for I have something very important to tell you." The bewildered people of Mecca gathered around the Prophet, and wondering what he was going to say, they began to ask, "O Muhammad! Why have you brought us here? What is this important news?"

When the Prophet was certain that he had the full attention of the crowd, he asked them, "If I were to tell you that behind this hill the enemy was waiting on horseback, ready to attack at any time, would you believe me?"

The people here had never known the Prophet to tell a lie; he was a man renowned for speaking the truth, so altogether the crowd called out, "Yes, we would believe you! For you have never spoken anything but the truth, you are Muhammad, the truthful one."

"Then I warn you that there is a great punishment awaiting all of you. Allah has commanded me: '*Warn your nearest kinsfolk'* of the grave torment of the Hereafter. *I am calling upon you to proclaim that there is no any other deity but Allah. There is eternal life after death*, and if you believe in Allah, you have nothing to fear! But if you reject faith in the one God, the flames of Hell await you. I am warning you all of the harsh punishment you will face."

The Prophet's uncle Abu Lahab began to shout from among the crowd, abusing the Prophet and throwing stones: "May you perish! Shame on you, is this why you gathered us here for?"

The Prophet left the crowd, and during the following days, he was subjected to severe torture from his uncle. Abu Lahab and his wife gathered thorns and branches from the mountains, and scattered them wherever the Prophet was certain to tread. Then the following verses of the Qur'an were revealed:

> *In the Name of Allah, the All-Merciful, the All-Compassionate. May both hands of Abu Lahab be perished, and he will perish! His wealth has not availed him, nor his gains. He will enter a flaming Fire to roast; and (with him) his wife, carrier of firewood (and of evil tales and slander). Around her neck will be a halter of strongly twisted rope.* (Tabbat 111:1–5)[3]

---

[3]   Bukhari, Ashab, 23; Salih Suruç, *Peygamberimizin Hayatı* (Life of the Prophet) Vol. 1, pp. 186–187.

The Other World

Abu Hurayra explained, "One day I went to see the Messenger of Allah, and he was performing the Prayer in the sitting position. When he finished praying, I asked him, 'O Messenger of Allah! Why are you sitting during the Prayer, are you ill?' and he replied, 'No, O Abu Hurayra, it is due to hunger.'

I began to weep, for the dearest servant of Allah, the cause for the creation of the universe, was praying sitting down because he had no strength to stand from extreme hunger.

When the Messenger of Allah saw me weeping he began to comfort me: 'O Abu Hurayra! Do not weep, for those (believers) who suffer from hunger in this world will be free from Divine punishment in the Hereafter.'"[4]

Throughout his life, the Messenger of Allah never once ate until he was full, not even if the meal was dry bread. On many occasions, days, weeks, and even months would pass without food being cooked in the Prophet's home (but they would just drink water and eat a few dates).[5]

---

4   Ali al-Muttaqi, *Qanzu'l-Ummal*, Vol. 7, p. 199.
5   Bukhari, Riqaq, 17; Muslim, Zuhd, 28.

Who Will Weep?

Abu Ubayda, one of the Companions of the Messenger, went to visit Umar during his caliphate. When he walked in and saw Caliph Umar weeping, Abu Ubayda asked, "O Caliph of the Faithful! Why are you weeping?"

Umar replied, "O Abu Ubayda! If I do not weep, then who will? The responsibility I have taken up is such that if a lamb was injured by the river of the Tigris, I would be held responsible. (On the Day of Judgment) Allah the Almighty will first question me for my own soul, and then for the people whom I govern. So tell me, if I do not have the right to weep, then who does?"[6]

The First Muslims Come to the Fore

It was the morning of the Eid celebration. The Companions began to gather at Umar's home to exchange greetings. Noticing the growing crowds, Caliph

---

[6] Ahmet Şahin, *Aradığımız Islam* (The Islam We Seek) p. 64; Ahmet Kurucan and Z. Mercan, *Cennetle Müjdelenen On Sahabi* (The Ten Companions Promised Paradise), p. 35.

Umar said: "Let the first to embrace Islam come to the fore, and the others form a line."

So those present formed a line according to when they accepted faith; Abu Sufyan was one of those present, but because he had embraced Islam much later, he was among the last group towards the end of the line. After a while, he became very agitated and began mumbling to himself, "Why should I have to wait here?"

Noticing Abu Sufyan's distress, Suhayl ibn Amr turned to him and said, "O Abu Sufyan! We all received the call to faith at the same time. But as you can see, because we refused to embrace Islam from the very beginning, we are at the end of the queue. You are agitated just because you have had to wait here for some time, so can you imagine what will happen if we are left until the end on the Day of Judgment." Suhayl ibn Amr's words affected Abu Sufyan immensely, and tears began to run down both men's cheeks.[7]

If I Am Refused Entrance

One day, Ibrahim ibn Adham, who was once a prince that renounced his throne to lead a devout, ascetic life, went to the public baths and asked the attendant, "I

---

[7]   Enes Selim, *Dini Hikayeler ve Kıssadan Hisseler* (Religious Stories and Their Morals), p. 72.

I Believe in the Hereafter

have no money, but will you allow me to enter the baths?" The attendant informed him that he would not allow anyone in without payment, and refused him entrance to the baths.

However much Ibrahim ibn Adham insisted on entering the baths, the attendant continued to refuse. So Ibrahim ibn Adham left totally demoralized, and outside the baths he began to lament in such distress that a crowd formed around him. When the people saw him weeping, they approached him and said, "Do not be sad, we will pay the fee for the baths, stop crying."

Ibrahim ibn Adham replied, "O people! Do you think I am crying because I could not enter the baths? This is not why I am crying. I was refused entrance to the baths because I had no money, but what will happen on the Day of Judgment if I am told 'Your deeds are insufficient to enter the Gardens of Paradise' and if I am refused entrance; this is what has upset me so much. Only those with good, righteous deeds, the ones who truly deserve Paradise, will be granted entrance."[8]

Divine Forgiveness and Paradise

And hasten, as if competing with one another, to forgiveness from your Lord, and to a Garden[9] as spacious as the heavens

---

[8] Ibrahim Sıddık Imamoglu, *Büyük Dini Hikayeler* (The Great Religious Stories), p. 261.

[9] While the promise for the "Gardens of Paradise" is given to those who believe and keep their duties to Allah and avoid sins out of

10

and the earth, prepared for the God-revering, pious. (Al 'Imran 3:133)

Know that the present, worldly life[10] is but a play, vain talk and ostentation, and mutual boasting among you, and competing in wealth and children – it is like when rain comes down and the vegetation grown by it pleases the farmers, (but) then it dries up and you see it turn yellow, then it becomes straw; and in the Hereafter there is a severe punishment, but also (there is) forgiveness from Allah and His good pleasure (which are everlasting); whereas the present, worldly life is but a transient enjoyment of delusion. And (rather than competing for the things of this world) race with one another to forgiveness from your Lord, and to a Garden the vastness of which

---

piety and reverence for Allah, "Divine forgiveness" precedes Paradise as stated in the verses above. This is due to the fact that Paradise is the place of perfect purity, and no one can enter Paradise without Divine grace and forgiveness. So before entering Paradise, Allah will clean or purify the people of Paradise of all their sins out of His pure grace, and the hardships they will have to suffer from resurrection to the gates of Paradise will also serve as a means of purification.

A believer should, therefore, always ask Allah for forgiveness for their sins and pray to Him, while also trying to be saved from sins and evils. In the words of Bediüzzaman Said Nursi, we should "take asking Allah for forgiveness for our sins in one of our hands, and prayer and worship in the other. Asking for forgiveness severs evils and sins from their roots, while prayer encourages doing good" (See Nursi, *The Words*, NJ: The Light, Inc., 2010, p. 485). (Ed.)

[10] The expression translated as *"the present, worldly life"* in the verse above refers not to the world itself but to the life that pertains to the bodily or material dimension of human existence. This is because the world is the field of testing and trial—the field to be sown for harvest in the Hereafter, and is also the place where the Divine Names are manifested. (Ed.)

is as the vastness of heaven and earth, prepared for those who truly believe in Allah and His Messengers. That is Allah's bounty, which He grants to whom He wills. Allah is of tremendous bounty. (Al-Hadid 57:20–21)

Beware of Death, Umar

D uring his reign as caliph, Umar was so afraid of unconsciously being unjust that he hired a clerk with his own money to constantly remind him of death. The clerk would come to Umar every day and say, "Beware of death, Umar!" and then leave. The clerk accompanied Umar wherever he went, reminding the caliph of death constantly throughout the day.

One day, the clerk entered and warned Umar, "Beware of death, Umar," and the caliph told his devoted employee, "I am dismissing you from your duty."

The clerk, puzzled, inquired, "O Umar! This is part of your daily routine, why are you abandoning such an excellent habit?"

Umar answered, "My beard now has streaks of white, and this is sufficient to remind me of death wherever I go; thus, I no longer require your warning."[11]

---

[11] Enes Selim, *Dini Hikayeler ve Kıssadan Hisseler* (Religious Stories and Their Morals), p. 211.

Three Things

Prophet Muhammad, peace and blessings be upon him, said, "Three things follow a person after death: his possessions, his family and his deeds. Two of them, the possessions and family, return from the grave, but his deeds remain with him."[12]

The Human Adventure

Summarizing the human journey through life, Ibrahim Hakki of Erzurum stated as follows:

"There are four realms or stages that a human lives through; the womb, life in this world, the intermediate realm of the grave, and life in the Hereafter. Every stage presents a different process of life, and of course, a different wisdom.

Just like an unborn child who has no aspiration to come into this world, a human has no desire to depart from this world. Like the newborn child who, recognizing the pleasure of his mother's milk, has no desire of returning to the

---

[12] Bukhari, Riqaq, 42; Muslim, Zuhd, 5; Tirmidhi, Zuhd, 46; Nasai, Janaiz, 52; Musnad Ahmad, Vol. 3, p. 110; Osman Oral, *100 Soruda Ahiret Hayatı* (Afterlife in 100 Questions), p. 100.

womb, the human who reaches their Lord after death has no desire of returning to this world."[13]

---

[13] Ibrahim Hakkı (of Erzurum), *Marifetname*, Vol. 1, p. 60.

The Last Breath
and the Ultimate Union

A Believer Longs to Meet Allah

T he Qur'an states, *"The stupor of death comes in truth (being the established decree of Allah for life). That is what (most people, especially the unbelievers and evildoers) are trying to flee from"* while the pious yearn to meet their Lord (Qaf 50:19).

Our beloved Prophet said, "At the moment of death, a believer is given the glad tidings of Allah's pleasure and His rewards. Therefore, there is nothing dearer to him than death, for he loves to meet Allah and Allah loves to meet him. But a disbeliever abhors the thought of death (and the following meeting with the Almighty for his or her judgment)."[14]

No Second Chance or Escape from Judgment

Will we, when we die and have become dust and bones – will we then really be (raised and) put under judgment? (As-Saffat 37:53)

---

[14] Bukhari, Riqaq, 41; Muslim, Dhikr, 14; Tirmidhi, Janaiz, 67.

Those who disbelieve claim that they will never be raised from the dead. Say: "Yes indeed, by my Lord, you will certainly be raised from the dead, then you will certainly be made to understand all that you did (in the world and called to account for it)." That is easy for Allah. (At-Taghabun 64:7)

A s stated in the verses above, some people claim that they will never be raised from the dead, and thus deny the following *"Promised Day (of Judgment)"*[15] while some others argue that their souls will live again in another body after their death.

Death is, indeed, only the end of this worldly life and there is no returning back in any form. There is, thus, no such thing as the rebirth of the soul in another body through reincarnation, transmigration of souls, or avatar bodies while in this world. Allah the Almighty says in the Qur'an, *"(No one will live forever!) Every soul is bound to taste death. So (O people) you will but be repaid in full on the Day of Resurrection (for whatever you have done in the world)."* (Al 'Imran 3:185)

So, everyone will be raised again to life from their "graves" to face judgment on the Day of Resurrection regardless of whether they were burnt into ashes, lost in the open space, mummified, or buried in the soil or the sea.

Those who persistently insist on denying the one and only God and His judgment on the Day of Reckoning, such as the Pharaohs who mummified their bodies in the hopes

---

[15]   Suratu'l-Buruj 85:2.

of eternalizing themselves, will abide forever in Hell as an afterlife of punishment.

They will beg for another chance to return back to the world, which is no more than a vain desire:

> If you could but see those disbelieving criminals when they hang their heads before their Lord (pleading): "Our Lord! Now we have seen and heard (the truth and are ready to be obedient). So return us (to the world): we will certainly do good, righteous deeds. Now we are certain (of the truth)." (As-Sajdah 32:12)

> "If only we might return to the world..." Thus does Allah show them their deeds in a manner that will cause them bitter regrets. Never will they come out of the Fire. (Al-Baqarah 2:167)

> They will wish to come out of the Fire, but they shall not come out of it; theirs is a punishment enduring. (Al-Maedah 5:37)

The following verses of the Qur'an decisively reject any doctrine or assertion of reincarnation which claims that people will be given chances to return to the world in new, different bodies so that they are purified of their sins. Instead of returning, the verses explicitly state that they will be brought before the Almighty to be judged:

> Have they not considered how many a generation We have destroyed before them; they never return to them (nor to their life of the world). Instead, every generation, all without exception, will be arraigned before Us (for judgment). (Ya-Sin 36:31–32)

(Those who persist in their evil ways will not cease from their false attributions to Allah, and from their harsh reaction to believers) until when death comes to one of them, and then he implores: "O my Lord! Please, let me return to life, that I may act righteously with respect to whatever I have left undone in the world."

No, never! It is merely a word that he utters over and over again. Before those (people who are dead) is an intermediate world (of the grave, where they will stay) until the Day[16] when they will be raised up. Then, when the Trumpet (of Resurrection) is blown, there will no longer be any ties of kinship among them (which will be of any avail), nor will they ask about one another (as everyone will be too engrossed in their own plight to think of others). (Scales of justice are set up to weigh a person's good and evil deeds,) and those whose scales (of good, righteous deeds) are heavy – they are the prosperous. While those whose scales are light – they will

---

[16] The Qur'an uses the word "day" not only in the sense of our normal day, but also as time unit and period. Therefore, the time when we are raised to life after death and judged, and eternally recompensed for what we did in this world, is referred to as a "day" (*Yawm*) in the Qur'an. That day is the time when the realities of religion will become clearly and fully manifest. This is one of the reasons why the Qur'an refers to that "day" as *Yawm ad-Dîn*, or the Day of Judgment. (See Ünal, *The Qur'an with Annotated Interpretation*, 2008, p. 6).

In the Qur'an, this "day" is also known as the Day of Reckoning (*Yawm al-Hisâb*), the Day of Recompense (*Yawm al-Jaza'*), the Day of Judgment and Distinction between people (*Yawm al-Fasl*), the Last Day (*Yawm al-Âkhirah*), the Promised Day (*Yawm al-Maw'ûd*), and the Hour (*as-Sâ'ah*). In addition, the term "*Yawm al-Ba'th*" is used for the Day of Rising while the term "*Yawm al-Qiyâmah*" is used for the Day of destruction of the world and the following Resurrection. (Ed.)

be those who have ruined their own selves, in Hell abiding.
(Al-Mu'minun 23:99–103)

The Last Breath

R elating to the last breath of an ill person, our beloved Prophet said, "Encourage the ill to recite *'Lâ ilâha illa'llâh'* (There is no deity but Allah) at the time of death.[17] Whoever recites *'Lâ ilâha illa'llâh'* (There is no deity but Allah), with their last breath is sure to enter Paradise."[18]

The Prophet also said, "When you are with an ill or dead person, speak well, for the angels are sure to say 'Amen' to whatever you say about them.[19] Recite Surah Ya-Sin of the Qur'an near the sick at the time of their death.[20]

Asking for Death

T he Prophet went to visit his uncle Abbas while he was ill, and when the Prophet heard his uncle complaining of his illness and asking for death, he said:

---

[17] Muslim, Janaiz, 1; Tirmidhi, Janaiz, 7; Abu Dawud, Janaiz, 20; Ibn Majah, Janaiz, 3.

[18] Tirmidhi, Janaiz, 7; Abu Dawud, Janaiz, 20.

[19] Muslim, Janaiz, 3; Abu Dawud, Janaiz, 19.

[20] Ibn Majah, Janaiz, 4.

"My dear uncle, do not ask for death! For if you are among the good and live, you will increase your good deeds in life; this will be better for you. But if you are a sinner, then you will have time to ask for Divine forgiveness and repent for your sins; this will also be better for you."[21]

"Blessed is the one whose life is long, and whose deeds commendable.[22] None of you should ever wish for death due to any misfortune that befalls them. If anyone is afflicted with such a severe adversity that they can no longer stand, then they should say, 'O Allah, grant me life for as long as living is better for me, and inflict me with death when death is better for me.'"[23]

The Eyes Weep and the Heart Grieves

The Prophet of Mercy, peace and blessings be upon him, wept at the death of his household members, including his wife Khadijah, his son Ibrahim, his daughter

---

21 Bukhari, Tamanni, 6.
22 Tirmidhi, Zuhd, 21–22; Darimi, Riqaq, 30; Musnad Ahmad, Vol. 2, pp. 235, 403; Vol. 5, p. 40.
23 Tirmidhi, Qiyamah, 26; Zuhd, 4; Nasai, Janaiz, 1; Musnad Ahmad, Vol. 2, p. 293.

and grandson,[24] and at the death of some of his Companions, including Uthman ibn Maz'un, and also during the illness of Saad ibn Ubadah. When the Prophet was reminded of the prohibition of mourning, he explained to his Companions that crying did not fall into the type of mourning that was forbidden, and there was no punishment for weeping for the dead; rather, the Divine punishment was for words and actions (such as wailing, becoming frantic with sorrow, complaining about Divine Destiny, tearing one's clothes or beating the chest) that displease Allah during times of affliction: "Surely, the deceased suffers torment for the wailing of their relatives.[25] The eye may weep, and the heart may grieve, but say nothing that displeases Allah!"[26]

The Earth Will Reject Him

There was a man from the People of the Book who embraced Islam and later became one of the scribes of the coming Revelations. This man later abandoned Islam; he told his friends, "Muhammad knows only that which I have written for him." When the man died, his

---

24 Bukhari, Janaiz, 32, 42; Ibn Majah, Janaiz, 53.
25 Bukhari, Janaiz, 43; Muslim, Janaiz, 6.
26 Bukhari, Janaiz, 32, 42–43.

friends and family buried him. But the next morning, to their surprise they saw that his body had been thrown back by the earth. They began to slander the Prophet, saying, "This is the act of Muhammad and his Companions; they dug him up and stole his shroud because he abandoned them."

Once again, they dug a grave, this time even deeper, and buried the man. The next morning, when they saw the body lying on top of the earth, they started to blame the Muslims again. This time they dug a grave as deep as they possibly could. On the third morning when they saw the body lying on the grave, they finally realized that this was not the act of human beings, so they left the body on top of the grave.

Long before the death of this apostate, the Prophet had said, "When this man dies, the earth will reject him."[27]

The First to Be United

Fatima, the dearest daughter of the blessed Prophet, died when she was twenty-nine years old. She died in the eleventh year of the migration to Medina, and only six months after the death of her father. She was the

---

[27] Bukhari, Manaqib, 25; Musnad Ahmad, Vol. 3, p. 121.

first of the blessed household to be united with her dear father, the Prophet.

Describing her death, Umm Salama said, "At the time of Fatima's death, (her husband) Ali was not at home. She called me and said, 'Can you prepare some water! I am going to bathe and put on clean clothing.' So I prepared her bath water and clothing and then she got dressed, and said: 'Can you get my bed ready, I am going to lie down.' I did as she asked, and Fatima turned her bed towards the *qiblah*.

Lying on the bed she said, 'O Umm Salama! The time has come. I have performed the rituals of purification, so having me performing the ritual bath a number of times and rubbing my body thoroughly will not be necessary.' Shortly after this the Prophet's dear daughter Fatima departed from the mortal world."[28]

The Anguish of Death

Amr ibn As, one of the Companions of the blessed Prophet, was on his death bed. When he was asked what death felt like, he replied, "I feel as if there is a thorn in my throat, and an enormous mountain on my

---

[28] S. Z. Dayıoglu, *Asrı Saadetten Tablolar* (Scenes from the Age of Bliss), p. 234.

shoulders! It's like the Heavens are caving in on top of me."[29]

The Fire-worshipper Who Honored Ramadan

One year during Ramadan the child of a fire-worshipper who lived in a neighborhood consisting mainly of Muslims stood out in the street eating bread among the fasting people. The boy was too young to understand Ramadan, or that the Muslims fasted during this holy month. But noticing the boy eating, his father rushed over saying, "Son, do you think it is right to eat in front of the Muslims? They are fasting, this month is very sacred and important to them." He sent the boy home.

One day this man, like all other mortal beings, died. After his death many of the men of wisdom in the city saw the fire-worshipper in their dreams; he was a resident of Paradise. Amazed at what they saw, the Muslims asked him in their dream, "We thought you were a disbeliever! We even refused to perform the Funeral Prayer after your death. How have you attained such a status?"

---

[29] Tirmidhi, Janaiz, 7–8; Abu Dawud, Janaiz, 20.

The man replied, "Yes, it is true that I was a worshipper of fire. But one day my young son was outside eating bread while the Muslims of the neighborhood were fasting. I ran over and stopped him from eating. Allah had mercy on me, and I submitted my soul as a Muslim, for I had sincere respect for anything the Muslims respected. So Allah commanded the Angel of Death to come to me; he told me to recite: '*Ashhadu an lâ ilâha illa'llâh wa ashhadu anna Muhammadan abduhû wa Rasûluh*' (I bear witness that there is no deity save Allah, and I bear witness that Muhammad is the servant and Messenger of Allah). I then submitted my soul to the angel. This is how I attained the blessing of abode in Paradise."[30]

An Old Sock

As his last will, a rich man asked his son, "The only thing I ask from you is that when I die, put an old sock on one of my feet!" So when the man died and the preparations were being made to wash the body, his son went to the imam and informed him of his father's wish, "We must put an old sock on one of my father's feet."

---

[30] Ibrahim Sıddık Imamoglu, *Büyük Dini Hikayeler* (The Great Religious Stories), p. 211; Enes Selim, *Dini Hikâyeler ve Kıssadan Hisseler* (Religious Stories and Their Morals), p. 75.

The imam told him, "According to Islamic regulations, I cannot allow the body to be covered in anything but a shroud." However, the man insisted that he be allowed to put an old sock on his father's foot and fulfill his last wish. So they gathered the wise and knowledgeable people of the city, and between them, they disputed the subject.

As the dispute continued, a man entered and gave the dead man's son a letter. The deceased man had written a letter to his son before his death. He began to read the letter aloud:

"My dear son, as you can see, although I have left so much wealth behind, I could not take any of it with me, not even an old sock. One day you too will die, just like me and every other mortal being. So be mindful of where and how you spend the wealth I left you, for when you die the only thing they will give you is a few meters of white cloth. Never forget that the only thing you will take to the grave is your good, righteous deeds, so act accordingly."

The scholars ruled that it was not possible to be buried with anything but the shroud. So they buried the man with nothing but a shroud of white cloth, and the deeds he performed in this world.[31]

31 Enes Selim, *Dini Hikayeler ve Kıssadan Hisseler* (Religious Stories and Their Morals), p. 78.

Very Soon

Mawlana Jalaluddin Rumi's dear wife told him, "It would take a saintly scholar as knowledgeable as you maybe three or four hundred years to fill the entire world with truth and wisdom." To which Rumi replied, "Why do you say such a thing? I am neither the Pharaoh nor Nimrod! This world is not a place to lastingly stay, and I am not interested in the pleasures of this mortal world. How can we possibly find peace here? I have been imprisoned in this world only to save a few of my fellow prisoners. And I sincerely hope to be united with the Prophet, Allah's beloved one, very soon."[32]

An Expedition to the Hereafter

On his return to Istanbul from the Egypt Campaign, instead of going on a new military expedition himself, Ottoman Sultan Yavuz Selim ordered his governors to make preparations for an expedition against Rhodes which had turned notoriously into a nest of pirates in the Mediterranean Sea. Then the sultan told them, "There will be no more expeditions for me but the expedition to the Hereafter." A short while after this he died.[33]

---

[32] Mehmet Akar, *Mesel Ufku* (The Horizon of Stories with Morals), p. 102.

[33] Enes Selim, *Dini Hikayeler ve Kıssadan Hisseler* (Religious Stories and Their Morals), p. 131.

Life in the Grave

The Two Graves

One day Prophet Muhammad, peace and blessings be upon him, passed by two graves and said, "The deceased in these two graves are being punished for acts which are not regarded important by humans. One of them did not protect or clean himself against urine.[34]

---

[34] Islam attaches great importance to the cleanliness of the private area. The term *istinja* is used for cleaning the private parts thoroughly after relieving oneself by washing and wiping the private parts. It should be kept in mind that washing the private area with water is superior to simply wiping the filthy area. This is due to the fact that water cleans it better. Indeed, cleaning the private parts with water and using toilet paper to dry the private parts is certainly the best way.

As for cleansing after urination, one must also ensure that there are no drops of urine, for the emission of any urine after making the ablution, no matter how small the amount, invalidates the ablution. Some scholars have said that people who do not pay attention to this, even though they know the importance of the issue, are like those who deliberately perform Prayers without ablution. In particular, men must be very sensitive about *istibra* (taking care that the flow of urine has fully ceased before making ablution). Therefore, it is not recommended to urinate in a standing position unless you have a valid excuse. Urinating in a sitting position is the best way. For in this way the bladder empties more

And the other used to destroy the relations of others with his gossip."

Then the Prophet took a fresh branch of a tree, broke it into two and planted a piece of the branch on each grave. When the Companions asked him what he was doing he replied, "I placed the branches in the hope that until these branches dry out their torment will be alleviated and that they will continue to ask forgiveness from Allah."[35]

Those Not Questioned in the Grave

Referring to those who will not be questioned in the grave, the Messenger of Allah, peace and blessings be upon him, said: "Those who will not be questioned in the grave are the Prophets, the martyrs, those who strive

---

easily. This will reduce dripping and leakage of urine. Thus, after a man has relieved himself, he should wait until the urine stops completely and make sure that none of it has fallen onto his clothes before he starts making the ablution. In order to be sure on this matter men can adopt such habits as coughing, taking a brisk walk, gently pressing one's penis, placing a tissue in one's underwear, and so on. In short, one must not only avoid any urine spattering on their clothes but also wait for the release of urine to come to an end so that no urine droplet spills on the body or garments. (Ed.)

[35] Bukhari, Wudu, 57; Janaiz, 79.

in all sincerity for the cause of Allah, those who die on a Friday (day or night), those who die of a stomachache, those who recite the Suratu'l-Mulk every night, and those unaccountable for their actions (such as young children and the insane)."[36]

Suratu'l-Mulk

Ibn Abbas explained, "One of the Companions unknowingly set up his tent on a grave. The Companion heard the deceased man in the grave reciting the Suratu'l-Mulk until he had completed the entire chapter. The Companion went to the Prophet and told him, 'O Messenger of Allah! I set my tent up on a grave unaware that it was a grave, and I heard the man in the grave reciting the Suratu'l-Mulk until he had completed the entire *surah*.' The Messenger of Allah replied, 'That *surah* is a protector! That *surah* is a savior; it saves one from the torment of the grave.'"[37]

---

[36] Muslim, Imarah, 50; Tirmidhi, Janaiz, 72–73, 112; Sawabu'l-Qur'an, 9; Nasai, Janaiz, 3–11.

[37] Tirmidhi, Sawabu'l-Qur'an, 9; Janaiz, 72.

Standing Guard

"Everyone who dies will have completed their deeds, except those who die while keeping guard for the sake of Allah, for their deeds will be increased until the Day of Judgment and they will be saved from the torment of the grave."[38]

The Dead Exposed to Their Abode in the Grave

Prophet Muhammad, peace and blessings be upon him, said, "The soul of a believer is a bird that feeds on the fruits of Paradise, until Allah returns the soul to its body on the Day of Resurrection. It (the believer's soul in the intermediate realm of the grave) sees the Paradise.[39]

The grave is either a garden of the gardens of Paradise, or a pit of the pits of Hell.[40] When one of you dies they are exposed to their abode in their graves morning and evening.[41] If they are among the residents of Paradise, they

---

[38] Tirmidhi, Jihad, 2; Musnad Ahmad, Vol. 2, p. 404.

[39] Ibn Majah, Zuhd, 32; Muwatta, Janaiz, 16; Nasai, Janaiz, 117.

[40] Tirmidhi, Qiyamah, 26.

[41] The grave is an intermediate world between this world and the Hereafter. The dead are exposed to a life resembling either Paradise or Hell, each according to their rank, in their graves until the

will be exposed to their abode in Paradise. If they are among those of Hell, they will be exposed to their abode in Hell and be told: 'This is where you are to remain until your resurrection on the Day of Judgment.'"[42]

The Grave as a Pit of Hell or a Garden of Paradise

Hasan al-Basri, who was a scholar from the second generation after the Prophet and one of the most eminent people in asceticism and knowledge, noticed a young girl standing by the grave of her father; she was crying, "O father! Every night I put you to bed, but who will help you now? I fed you every night, but who will feed

---

Resurrection. If a believer leads a virtuous life in the world, windows onto heavenly scenes will be opened for them, and their grave will become like a garden of Paradise. Unbelievers who indulge in sin will see scenes of Hell, and their graves will become like a pit of Hell. (See Ünal, *The Qur'an with Annotated Interpretation*, p. 720). The Qur'an mentions, for instance, the punishment of the Fire for the Pharaoh and his court in the grave in the form of being exposed to it in the morning and evening: *"The Fire: they are exposed to it morning and evening; and when the Last Hour comes in (and the Judgment is established, it is ordered): 'Admit the clan of the Pharaoh into the severest punishment.'"* Therefore, while the Pharaoh and his clan will be exposed to the Fire in their graves morning and evening, their punishment in Hell will be in the form of continuous burning. (Ed.)

[42] Tirmidhi, Janaiz, 70.

you now?" So Hasan Basri walked over to the girl and said, "My dear! What you should be asking is this: Father, we placed you in the grave facing the *qiblah*, have you turned away? Does your grave resemble the gardens of Paradise or the dungeons of Hell? Are you able to answer the angels who are questioning you?"[43]

After Death

The Prophet was asked, "O Messenger of Allah! Is there any duty I can perform after my parents die?" The Prophet replied, "Yes, you can pray for them, ask Allah for forgiveness of their sins, fulfill their wills, maintain relations with their relatives by visiting them, and honor their friends."[44]

A Gift to the Souls of the Grave

During the time of Hasan al-Basri, a woman came to him and said, "O Imam! I had a young daughter who died a few months ago. I miss her so much, and

---

[43] Ahmet Coşkun, *Eskimeyen Hikayeler* (Timeless Stories), p. 12.
[44] Abu Dawud, Adab, 129; Ibn Majah, Adab, 2.

although I grieve for her so deeply, I have not seen her, not even once in a dream, since she died. Could you teach me a prayer so I could at least see my beloved daughter in my dream, and find some kind of comfort from this overwhelming grief?"

So Hasan al-Basri taught the woman a prayer, and sent her home. The woman recited the supplication exactly as the imam had taught her, and after pleading with Allah, she went to bed with tears rolling down her cheeks. The woman did eventually see her daughter, but greatly regretted it, for the young girl was subjected to torment, and this caused the woman great distress. The girl was enrobed in a garment of flames and suffering harsh punishment.

Greatly affected by her dream, the woman awoke, and early the next morning returned to Hasan al-Basri and told him her dream. She asked him how she could save her daughter from the torment of the grave, and which deeds she could perform so that her daughter might be forgiven for her sins.

Hasan al-Basri advised the woman what to do, and sent her home. But a short time after, Hasan al-Basri had a dream. In this dream a young, beautiful girl was sitting on a golden throne. Rays of light were beaming from around her. The girl asked Hasan al-Basri, "Do you know who I am?" When he replied that he had no idea who she was, asking which of the Prophet's daughters or wives she was, the girl answered: "I am the daughter of the woman who came to you for advice, the girl whom she saw in her dream in a state of torment. And she asked what she should do to attain forgiveness for my sins." Totally surprised, Hasan al-Basri said, "But your mother told me that you were enduring harsh torture; what has saved you from the Divine punishment?"

The girl replied, "O Imam! One of the beloved servants of Allah passed through the graveyard, recited Suratu'l-Fatiha and Suratu'l-Ikhlas three times, he prayed to Allah for the bestowal of blessings upon the Prophet and his family three times, and then bestowed these recitations as a gift to the souls of the graves. All of a sudden we heard a voice saying: 'Relieve those suffering torment in this graveyard.' There were five hundred and fifty souls, including mine, that were saved from the Divine punishment and granted the pleasures of Paradise."

Hasan al-Basri explained his dream to the woman, and gave her the glad tidings that her daughter had been saved from the torments of the grave. He then advised the woman to frequently pray for the bestowal of blessings upon the noble Prophet and his family (for the sake of whom Allah would deliver them from the torments of the grave).[45]

---

[45] *Evliyalar Ansiklopedisi* (Encyclopedia of the Saints), See the entry for Hasan al-Basri, Istanbul: Türkiye Gazetesi, p. 233.

Do You Remember?

Islamic scholar Shibli died and a short time after, one of his companions saw him in a dream and asked, "How are you?"

Explaining what happened after his death, Shibli replied, "I was forgiven by Allah, and standing before Him when He asked, 'Do you know why I forgave you?' I answered, 'O Allah! I presume that You forgave me for my Prayers and regular fasting.' But Allah replied in the negative, as both the Prayers and fasting were my duty as a believer.

Allah the Almighty then informed me of the action that pleased Him, 'O Shibli! Do you remember when you were walking in the street one day and you came across a cat shivering from the cold. You pitied the cat so much that you took it home, and warmed it up?' I replied, 'O Lord! Yes, I remember.' Then Allah told me, 'It is because of this very action of yours that I forgave you for your mistakes, O Shibli!'"[46]

The Account of a Rope

A very wealthy man was so afraid of death and the isolation of the grave that he said, "I will give half of my wealth to whoever accompanies me to the grave on the night I die until morning."

---

[46] Enes Selim, *Dini Hikayeler ve Kıssadan Hisseler* (Religious Stories and Their Morals), p. 102; *Hikayelerle Din Egitimi* (Stories for Religious Education), p. 231.

So when the man died, they asked who would spend the night in the grave with the rich man; only one man agreed to do so. The man, a porter who carried loads for a living, thought to himself, "I have nothing to lose but this piece of rope; if I accompany the man in the grave until dawn, I will become rich." So the man agreed and they buried him along with the deceased, making a hole so that he could breathe. When the Angels of Reckoning came, they noticed that there was a living man beside the body of the deceased.

So they conferred among themselves, finally saying, "This dead man is a sure thing for the questioning anyway. So, let's leave him for now and question the other man." Thus they began questioning first the man who was alive: "Whose rope is that? Where did you get it? Why did you buy it? With what means did you obtain it? What do you use it for?" And although the questioning continued until dawn, the man's account was still incomplete. When he finally climbed out of the grave, those present said, "You accompanied this man in the grave, so you deserve half of his wealth." The man replied, "God forbid! I refuse to take any of his wealth. I was unable to give account for a mere piece of rope, how could I possibly answer for all that wealth?"[47]

---

[47]   Mehmet Akar, *Mesel Denizi* (The Ocean of Stories with Morals), Istanbul: Nil Yayınları, 2001, p. 156.

In Honor of a Letter

Exactly one year after Umar's death, his son Abdullah had a dream in which Umar appeared; his face looked so white that Abdullah asked, "O father! Why are you so white and drained?" Umar replied, "My son! I have been giving account to Allah for my actions for a year, I have only just completed my questioning; that is why I am so tired and look so pale."

Abdullah asked, "Father! How was your questioning?" Umar replied, "As one account ended another began; if I did not have the letter that I asked to be placed in my shroud with me before I was buried, it most certainly would have been much worse. Do you remember when the reins of Shirin (one of the relief camels) grew worn, and after tying and repairing the reins many times, we eventually disposed of them. I was held for account for those reins, and scolded by Allah: 'By casting those reins away, you wasted the property of the Muslims.' There was nothing I could say. I was saved only thanks to that letter."

Explaining the details of the letter, Abdullah said, "One day during his caliphate, Hasan and Husayn came to visit my father. He gave them a gown each; this pleased them very much. When Ali saw the new gowns, he too was delighted and said, 'Go and inform Caliph Umar that the Messenger of Allah said: 'In this world, Umar is the light of Islam, and after his death he will be the light of the residents of Paradise.' So my father asked them to write this on a piece of paper, which they did. Then my father told me, 'When I die, place this paper in my shroud so that it will accompany me to the grave. And when I find myself in any difficulty, I will show this letter and reach salvation.'"[48]

---

[48] Enes Selim, *Dini Hikayeler ve Kıssadan Hisseler* (Religious Stories and Their Morals), p. 79.

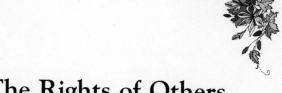

The Rights of Others

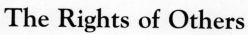

The Rights of Man Are
unlike Anything Else

Whenever he walked down a road or pathway, Umar would remove stones and clear the paths of anything that could be potentially harmful to others. One day he noticed a stone and kicked it to the side of the road. Rolling to the roadside, the stone hit the foot of one of the Companions. This upset Umar very much and repeatedly apologized for the accident, but there was nothing he could do.

A year passed, and once again Umar was clearing stones from the road; he was in the same place where he had accidently hit the Companion's foot a year earlier. Just then he noticed the same Companion passing, so the caliph took a pouch of gold coins from his pocket and gave them to the man saying, "Take this money and spend it."

The man looked at Umar in total amazement and said, "O, Commander of the Faithful, I have money!" Umar replied, "I know you have money, but I want you to accept it." "This is not necessary O Umar! I do not need the money," the man responded.

Umar then asked, "Do you intend to perform Hajj this year?" "Yes, God willing," he replied. "Then take this and spend it on your journey," Umar said. "But I already have the money for my journey," the man replied. When Umar said, "I know you have enough money for the journey; I want you to take this and forgive me for what I did," the man asked, "O, Commander of the Faithful, forgive you for what?"

Then Umar said, "Last year, while I was clearing this road of stones, one of the stones I kicked to the roadside hit your foot by accident. The fact that I hit one of the people of Medina with a stone, even if it was accidently, has caused me great distress. So I have decided to give you this gold to relieve myself of this sadness, and also as a token of your forgiveness. If you accept and forgive me, you will make me a very happy man. As you know, the rights of a human being are unlike anything else on earth."

Until a Debt Is Paid

Prophet Muhammad, peace and blessings be upon him, refused to perform the Funeral Prayer for a man who had died with debt. He only performed the Prayer when one of those present agreed to pay the debts of the deceased man. The Prophet then said, "The soul of a believer is held hostage by his debt, and the torment in the grave continues until the debt is paid."[49]

Punishment for a Woodchip

While Prophet Jesus, peace be upon him, was walking past a grave, he saw the deceased suffering the Divine punishment, and asked his Lord the reason for this man's torment. He received the following answer: "O Jesus! Pray that My servant may be resurrected, that you may ask him yourself why he was subjected to such a punishment."

So Jesus prayed and when the deceased came before Jesus, he inquired why the man was being punished. The man answered, "O Jesus! Before I died, I carried loads for a living. One day while I was carrying wood for somenoe, I snapped off a small woodchip to pick my tooth without asking permission from the owner. This is the reason for my punishment." Then the man returned to the grave.[50]

---

49   Ibn Majah, Sadaqat, 12.
50   S. Z. Dayıoglu, *Peygamberler Tarihi* (History of the Prophets), Vol. 3, p. 256.

The Rights of Others

Prophet Muhammad, peace and blessings be upon him, said that the account regarding the rights of others will be very harsh: "Whoever has violated another person's rights, regarding their honor or anything else, should ask for forgiveness (from the person) before the Day of Judgment. If they fail to do this, any good deeds they may have will be taken from them according to the violation which they have committed and given to the person whose rights they violated. But if they have no good deeds, then the sins of the person will be removed and added to their account."[51]

---

[51] Bukhari, Mazalim, 10, Riqaq, 48; Tirmidhi, Qiyamah, 2.

The Resurrection and the Day of Judgment

Blasts of the Trumpet
and the Revival

(The Last Hour will have come) on the Day when a blast (of the Trumpet) will convulse (the world), followed by the succeeding one.[52] *Hearts on that Day will be throbbing in distress; the eyes downcast. Yet, they (the unbelievers) say: "Will we really be restored to our former state (of life)? Will we when we have become bones rotten and crumbled away?" They say (in derision): "Then, that would be a return with*

---

[52] As revealed in various verses of the Qur'an, the end of the world will come when the earth will be shaken with a violent blast of the Trumpet. The Resurrection is when human beings will rise from their graves with the second blast of the Trumpet to stand before their Creator for judgment. All the dead revived with the second blast will then hasten toward the Plain of Supreme Gathering: *"The Day when they come forth from their graves in haste as if they were hurrying to a goal"* (Al-Ma'arij 70:43).

The unbelievers who will witness the destruction of the world will also be greatly shaken by the second blow of the Trumpet and revival. Thus, the unbelievers will come to understand the truth of the Day of Judgment, and everything about it will be revealed to them. Indeed, on this Day of Judgment, every human, believers and unbelievers alike, will be given their book of deeds and judged before the Supreme Court, and their deeds will be weighed on the scales of justice. (Ed.)

loss!" It will indeed be but a single cry, and then, they will all have been awakened to life on the plain (of Supreme Gathering). (An-Nazi'at 79:6–14)

The Trumpet will be blown, and so all who are in the heavens and all who are on the earth will fall dead, except those whom Allah wills to exempt. Then it will be blown for the second time, and see, they have all stood upright, looking on (in anticipation). (Az-Zumar 39:68).

On the Day when the Trumpet is blown all who are in the heavens and all who are on the earth will be stricken with shock and terror, except those whom Allah wills to exempt. All will come to His Presence, utterly humbled. (An-Naml 27:87)

Hearts Well-pleased with Allah and Well-pleasing to Him

Two of the Prophet's Companions, Abdullah ibn Abbas and Abdullah ibn Amr, ran into each other. Abdullah ibn Abbas asked, "Which verse from the Book of Allah gives you the most hope?" Abdullah ibn Amr replied with the verse, "*O My servants who have been wasteful against (the good of) their own souls! Do not despair of Allah's Mercy. Surely Allah forgives all sins. He is indeed the All-Forgiving, the All-Compassionate*" (Az-Zumar 39:53).

Abdullah ibn Abbas said, "For me it is the verse when Prophet Abraham said, '*My Lord, show me how You will*

restore life to the dead!' Allah said, 'Why? Do you not believe?'
Abraham said, 'Yes, (I most certainly do), but that my heart
may be at rest' (Al-Baqarah 2:260). And Allah the Almighty
was pleased with this reply of Prophet Abraham."

Then, Abdullah ibn Abbas concluded by saying, "Life
after death is an issue which Satan may exploit to whisper suspicion[53] into people's mind."[54]

The Tailbone

T he Messenger of Allah, peace and blessings be upon
him, explained that the re-creation of humankind
after death will begin with a bone, the size of a mus-
tard seed, called the tailbone. He said, "Allah will send
water from the Heavens and the dead bodies will grow

---

[53] Indeed, Satan is able to whisper his words of suspicion into the
human heart and mind, finally leading those ones he deceived into
further astray. The Qur'an brings such people to our attention as
in the following verses (which mean):

"*Will we, when we die and have become dust and bones — will we
then really be (raised and) put under judgment?*" (As-Saffat 37:53).

"*They (the unbelievers) say: 'Will we really be restored to our
former state (of life)? Will we when we have become bones rotten and
crumbled away?' They say (in derision): 'Then, that would be a
return with loss!' It will indeed be but a single cry, and then, they will
all have been awakened to life on the plain (of Supreme Gathering)*"
(An-Nazi'at 79:10–14). (Ed.)

[54] Ibn Kathir, *Tafsiru'l-Qur'an al-Azim*, Vol. I, p. 467.

like vegetation grows;[55] there is nothing in the human body that does not decay except one bone. This is the tailbone (or *'ajb adh-dhanab*[56] as called in the hadith) at the end of the spinal column, and it is from this that the human body will be recreated on the Day of Resurrection."[57]

Killing Death

A bu Said reported that the Messenger of Allah, peace and blessings be upon him, said, "On the Day of Resurrection, death will be brought in the form of

---

[55] The Qur'an says, "*And Allah has caused you to grow from earth like a plant (in a mode of growth particular to you). Thereafter He will return you into it (when you die), and He will bring you forth from it (again at the Resurrection).*" (Nuh 71:17–18)

[56] The grave is an intermediate world between this world and the next. After burial, the spirit waits in this intermediate world between this one and the Hereafter. Although the body decomposes, its essential particles (called *'ajb adh-dhanab*, which literally means tailbone or coccyx, in the hadith above) do not rot. The spirit continues its relations with the body through it. Our Lord, who is the All-Powerful and Ever-Able to do whatever He wishes, will make this part, which is formed of the body's essential particles, atoms, or all its other particles already dispersed in the soil, conducive to eternal life during the final destruction and rebuilding of the universe. He also will use it to re-create us on the Day of Judgment (See also Ünal, 2008, p. 720). (Ed.)

[57] Bukhari, Tafsir, 39/3; Muslim, Fitan, 141–142.

a black-and-white ram, and placed on the border between Heaven and Hell. Then a voice will call out, 'O residents of Paradise! Do you recognize this?' All the residents will raise their heads and look towards the ram, and answer, 'Yes, it is death!'

Then the same voice will ask the residents of Hell, 'O residents of the Hellfire! Do you recognize this?' All the inmates of Hell will raise their heads and look towards the ram, and answer, 'Yes, it is death!'

Then the ram will be slaughtered; again the voice will say, 'O residents of Paradise! Here is the eternal life, you will never die. O residents of the Hellfire! Here is the eternal life, you will never die.'" Then the Prophet recited the following verses (which mean):

> So warn people of the coming of the Day of anguish and regrets, the day when everything will have been decided, for (even now) they are in heedlessness, and they do not believe. Surely, it is We alone Who will inherit the earth and all who live on it; and to Us all will be brought back. (Maryam 19:39–40)[58]

Travelling on the Day of Judgment

Allah the Almighty reveals in the Qur'an, "*On the Day when He will assemble you all for the Day of Assembly – that will be the day of loss for some (the unbeliev-*

---

58 Bukhari, Jannah, 23; Muslim, Jannah, 78.

ers) and gain for some (the believers)" (At-Taghabun 64:9).
With respect to this Day, the Messenger of Allah, peace
and blessings be upon him, said, "People will assemble in
three groups on the Day of Judgment: those who walk, those
who ride, and others who crawl on their faces." Then someone asked, "O Messenger of Allah! How will they crawl
on their faces?"

The Prophet replied, "The One Who has the power to
make them walk on their feet also has the power to make
them crawl on their faces. But those who crawl on their
faces will try to protect themselves from every obstacle, or
thorn they encounter with their faces. Those who walk
will also face difficulties, but their difficulty will be much
lighter than the difficulties of the ones who crawl. The
most fortunate and honorable are those who ride. Those
who crawl on their faces are the disbelievers, as conveyed
in the following verse of the Qur'an (which means):

> *Whoever Allah guides, then he it is who is rightly guided; and
> whoever He leads astray, you shall find for them, apart from
> Him, no guardians (who might own and help them). We will
> raise them to life and gather them together on the Day of Res-
> urrection–prone upon their faces, blind, dumb, and deaf. Their
> refuge is Hell–every time it (seems to them that its torment) is
> abating (because of their being inured to it), We increase them
> in (suffering in its) blazing flame.* (Al-Isra 17:97).[59]

---

59   Tirmidhi, Tafsir Isra, 18.

The Supreme Court

Everyone will go to the Supreme Court alone and be questioned about their deeds. They will be aligned before their Lord, Who will tell them:

> Now assuredly you (having died and been buried alone) have come to us quite alone, as We created you in the first instance; and you have left behind all that We bestowed upon you (in the world). And We do not see with you any of those 'intercessors' (whom you associated with Allah as partners, and) of whom you supposed that they had shares in you (i.e. authority to order your life in certain ways). (Al-An'am 6: 94)

On the Day of Judgment, people will also be sorted out into the people of Paradise and the people of Hell. The people of Paradise will be in two main groups: those who are the nearest to Allah and the others.

> On the Day when He will assemble you all for the Day of Assembly – that will be the day of loss for some (the people of Hell) and gain for some (the people of Paradise). (At-Taghabun 64:9)

> On that day, all humans will come forth in different companies, to be shown their deeds (that they did in the world). And so, whoever does an atom's weight of good will see it; and whoever does an atom's weight of evil will see it. (Az-Zilzal 99:6–8)

So, every person will be shown all their deeds, down to the smallest ones. However, as Allah overlooks and forgives many of people's evils in the world, except unbelief and the association of partners with Him, He will also forgive some evils of His believing servants in the Hereafter.

The Account of Five Things

The Prophet explained that on the Day of Judgment the feet of a servant will not depart from the presence of their Lord until they have accounted for five things: Where they spent their lifespan, what (good and bad) deeds they committed in the world, how they earned and spent their wealth, how they utilized their youth, and how much they acted upon their knowledge.[60]

If the Account Is Complete

The Messenger of Allah, peace and blessings be upon him, said that the first question asked on the Day of Judgment would be regarding a person's faith. Those with faith will then be questioned about their deeds.

He then explained that following the question of faith, the first thing a human being will be accountable for will

---

60 Tirmidhi, Qiyamah, 1.

be their daily Prayers: "On the Day of Judgment, the first thing a person will be accountable for is their Prayers. If their account is complete, then they have reached salvation. If their account is incomplete, they will fall into detriment. If their obligatory Prayers are incomplete, Allah will command His angels: 'Look if My servant has any supererogatory Prayers.' Thus, their deficiency in Prayers will be completed with their supererogatory Prayers. Then they will be questioned about the remainder of their deeds in the same way."[61]

When a Human Dies

Prophet Muhammad, peace and blessings be upon him, said, "When a human dies, his deeds cease (to be recorded in their book of deeds), except for three things: his continuing (works of) charity, beneficial knowledge (that he has taught or authored and thus conveyed to others), and a righteous child who prays for him."[62]

---

[61] Tirmidhi, Salah, 305; Nasai, Salah, 9; Muwatta, Qasru's-Salah, 89.
[62] Muslim, Wasayah, 3; Abu Dawud, Wasayah, 14; Musnad Ahmad, Vol. 2, p. 372.

I Believe in the Hereafter

The Book of Deeds

eferring to how people will make excuses when
they stand before the Supreme Divine Court for
judgment and how their excuses will unavoidably
follow Allah's bringing forth for every individual a book
of deeds which will be spread open and dealt out, the
Prophet said, "People will stand before Allah three times
on the Day of Judgment. On the first two occasions,
they will make excuses. But on the third, the pages from
the book of deeds will begin to open. Some will receive
their book of deeds in their right hand, and some in
their left."[63]

So, everyone will receive a book that contains a record
of everything they committed during their lifetime in the
world. They will be told, *"Read your book! Your own self
suffices you this day as a reckoner against you."* (Al-Isra'
17:14)

The Qur'an also portrays the reaction of the people
when they receive their own book of deeds as follows:

> On that Day you will be arraigned for judgment, and no
> secret of yours will remain hidden. Then as for him who is
> given his Record in his right hand, he will say: "Here, take
> and read my Record! I surely knew that (one day) I would
> meet my account." And so he will be in a state of life pleas-
> ing to him, in a lofty Garden, with clusters (of fruit) within
> easy reach. "Eat and drink to your hearts' content for all

---

[63] Tirmidhi, Qiyamah, 5.

that you sent ahead in advance in days past (in anticipation of this Day)."

But as for him whose Record is given in his left hand, he will say: "Ah, would that I had never been given my Record and that I had known nothing of my account! Oh, would that death had been (and nothing thereafter had followed). My wealth has availed me nothing, and all my authority (my power over all that I had) has gone from me!" (And the command will come): "Lay hold of him and shackle him (by the neck, the hands, and the feet)! Then in the Blazing Flame let him to roast." (Al-Haqqah 69:18–31)

And the Record (of everyone's deeds) is set in place; and you will see the disbelieving criminals filled with dread because of what is in it, and they will say: "Alas, woe is ours! What is this Record? It leaves out nothing, be it small or great, but it is accounted!" They have found all that they did confronting them (in the forms thereof particular to the Hereafter). And Your Lord does not treat any one with injustice. (Al-Kahf 18:49)

Our beloved Prophet told his community to pray as follows while washing the left and right arms during ablution: "O Allah! Place me among those who receive the book of deeds in their right hand! Do not place me among those who receive the book of deeds in the left hand or from behind!"[64]

---

[64] Abu Dawud, Taharah, 48.

The Record of the Wicked

No indeed! The record of the shameless dissolute one is surely in sijjîn (a lowly register, portending eternal punishment). What enables you to perceive what sijjîn is? A register inscribed indelibly and sealed. Woe on that Day to those who deny—those who deny the Day of Judgment! (This is the Day) which none denies except everyone exceeding the bounds (set by Allah), everyone addicted to sinning, who, when Our Revelations are conveyed to him, says: "Fables of the ancients!" By no means! But what they themselves have earned has rusted upon their hearts (and prevents them from perceiving the truth). By no means! Assuredly they will on that Day be veiled from (the mercy of) their Lord. Then they will certainly enter in the Blazing Flame to roast. Thereafter they will be told: "This is what you used to deny (while in the world)." (Al-Mutaffifîn 83:7–17)

The Record of the Virtuous

No indeed! The record of the virtuous and godly ones is surely in 'illiyyîn (a lofty register, portending elevated stations). What enables you to perceive what 'illiyyîn is? It is a register inscribed indelibly and sealed. Those who are near-stationed to Allah will attest to it. The virtuous and godly ones will certainly be in (Gardens of) bounty and blessing; on thrones, looking around (at the blessings of Paradise). You will recognize on their faces the brightness of bliss. They will be served to drink pure wine under the seal (of Divine sanction and preservation). Its seal is a fragrance of musk. And to that (bless-

ing of Paradise), then, let all those who aspire (to things of high value) aspire as if in a race (with each other). Its admixture will be from tasnîm (the most delightful drink out of the loftiest spring of Paradise). A spring from which those near-stationed to Allah drink. (Al-Mutaffifîn 83:18–28)

Easy Reckoning

As for him who will be given his Record in his right hand, surely he will be reckoned with by an easy reckoning, and will return in joy to his household (prepared for him in Paradise).[65] But as for him who will be given his Record (in his left hand) from behind his back, he will surely pray for destruction, and enter the Flame to roast, for indeed he used to be in joyous conceit among his household (in his earthly life).[66] (Al-Inshiqaq 84:7–13)

---

[65] When believers are brought before the Supreme Court to account for their deeds, their evil acts will be forgiven if their good deeds outweigh their evil acts, and they will receive *"an easy reckoning."* They will also unite with their faithful household in the Hereafter: *"Those who have believed and their offspring have followed them in faith, We will unite them with their offspring"* (At-Tur 52:11). However, if somebody is called to a severe account, as stated in a Prophetic Tradition, this will mean his or her doom. (Bukhari, 'Ilm, 35; Muslim, Jannah, 80).

[66] As stated clearly in the verses above, the contrast between the state of a believer and an unbeliever is highly significant. An unbeliever condemned to the punishment of Hell is the one who is conceited and joyful among their household in the world. They rejoice in their worldly possessions, of which they are proud, and are indifferent to

The Final Meeting

When the Last Hour stands forth (and the Judgment is established) — on that Day, all people will be separated from one another. As for those who believe and do good, righteous deeds, they will be honored and made happy in a delightful Garden. But those who disbelieve and deny Our Revelations and the final meeting (with Us) in the Hereafter, such will be arraigned for punishment (in Hell). (Ar-Rum 30:14-16)

Did You Ever Consider?

Our beloved Prophet said, "The servant will be called to account on the Day of Judgment. Allah the Almighty will ask him, 'Did I not (bestow many favors upon you and) give you ears (to take heed), eyes

---

their Creator and His commands. When they see the punishment in the Hereafter, they will pray for eternal destruction. Whereas a believer who is to be rewarded with eternal bliss in the other world is the one who is very careful and alert among his or her family for their guidance and eternal life. (See Ünal, 2008, p. 1212). Pleased with what they will be given in the Hereafter, they will say, *"We used to be, when amongst our families, indeed most apprehensive before (most careful and alert for the guidance and eternal life of our family members). Then Allah bestowed His favor upon us, and protected us from the punishment of the scorching fire penetrating through the skin. We used to worship and invoke Him alone before. Surely He is the All-Benign, the All-Compassionate (especially to His believing servants)"* (At-Tur 52:26–28). (Ed.)

(to see the truth, and all of those) wealth and offspring? Did I not grant you ease in the care and maintenance of your animals and fields? Did I not create you superior to the whole of creation? Did you ever consider this meeting with Me?'

The servant will reply, 'No.' Then Allah will say, 'Thus, I will forget you today,[67] just how you forgot Me in the world.'"[68]

---

[67] The only thing the Almighty Allah has asked from His servants in return for all His blessings in this world is recognition of Him and expression of gratitude for all the blessings by remembrance and worship of Him. In the verse, *"Do not be like those who are oblivious of Allah and so Allah has made them oblivious of their own selves. Those, they are the transgressors"* (Al-Hashr 59:19), Allah the Almighty warns His servants not to be like those who are oblivious of Him. He tells them to the effect: You are oblivious and unaware of yourselves. You do not want to remember death although you see around that every human is bound to taste death. You do not like obeying Allah in your lives and follow your lusts and caprices, and so are oblivious of the purpose for your worldly life. To purify yourselves of this, carry out your responsibilities, be prepared for death, and forget whatever transient reward you might obtain in the world. You should never forget why you are here in the world and what you should do, and for what end you are heading. Otherwise, (a Day will come and) it will be said: *"We are oblivious of you today (so do not hope for forgiveness and favor), as you were oblivious of the encounter of this day of yours, and your (lasting) refuge will be the Fire, and you have no helpers"* (Al-Jathiya 45:34). (Ed.)

[68] Tirmidhi, Qiyamah, 7.

The Weight of the Scales of Justice

Our beloved Prophet said, "On the Day of Judgment, Allah will bring one of my followers from among all the people and spread before him ninety-nine registers (of his deeds). Each of them will be stretched as far as one can see. Then Allah the Almighty will ask His servant, 'Do you deny anything written? Have My angels that recorded your deeds treated you unjustly? The servant will reply, 'No, my Lord.'

Allah the Almighty will then ask him, 'Do you have any excuse?' The servant will say, 'No, my Lord.'

Then Allah the All-High will say, 'Behold! You have an accepted righteous deed in Our Presence. (Therefore,) We will not impose the punishment which is due for your faults today.' Then a slip will be taken out, upon which is written: "*Ashadu an lâ ilâha illa'llâh wa ashadu anna Muhammadan abduhû wa rasûluh*" (I bear witness that there is no deity but Allah, and I bear witness that Muhammad is the servant and Messenger of Allah). All the registers of his deeds will be placed on one side of the scale, and the slip (of his sincere profession of faith) on the other. The registers will be lighter in weight than the slip."[69]

---

[69] Tirmidhi, Iman, 17.

The Bridge over Hell

One day the Prophet explained the narrow Sirat bridge spanning across the dungeons of Hell to his Companions, saying, "The Sirat bridge will be laid across the Hellfire (to be crossed in order to enter Paradise). I will be the first among the Prophets to cross the bridge, accompanied by my followers. On either side of the bridge will be hooks of steel that resemble the thorns of a thistle. These hooks will take hold of people because of their evil deeds; some of them will perish, and some will fall off the bridge into the flames of Hell, but saved later.

When Allah desires to save those from the flames, He will bestow His Mercy and command the angels to remove those residents of the Fire who worshipped Him. The angels will recognize those who are to be saved by the marks of prostration, for Allah has prohibited the flames from burning those parts of body that prostrate in Prayer."[70]

A Dream

Caliph Umar ibn Abdulaziz was an extremely just and pious ruler who lived a very humble life. One day his servant had a dream, and requested permission to relate his dream to the caliph.

---

[70] Bukhari, Riqaq, 52; Tawhid, 24; Muslim, Iman, 299; Tirmidhi, Jannah, 20.

"O, Commander of the Faithful! I saw the Day of Judgment in my dream. The people were ordered to cross the Sirat; some reached the other side, while others were not so fortunate. The caliphs who reigned before you were the next to cross the bridge. First they told Abdulmalik ibn Marwan to cross, but I saw him fall over the side of the bridge. Then they ordered the other caliphs to cross the bridge, some reached the other side, while others failed. Eventually, it was your turn." But before the servant had the chance to continue, Umar ibn Abdulaziz began to shout "O Allah!"

In a state of total astonishment, the servant said, "O, Commander of the Faithful! I swear by Allah, you crossed the bridge immediately." But Umar was so distraught and overcome with the awe of Allah that he was unable to hear his servant's words of reassurance.[71]

Pioneering to Cross the Bridge

A man asked our beloved Prophet, "On the Day of Judgment, where will the people be resurrected?" The Prophet replied, "(They will be on the Plain

---

71 Ibrahim Sıddık Imamoglu, *Büyük Dini Hikayeler* (The Great Religious Stories) p. 283; Enes Selim, *Dini Hikayeler ve Kıssadan Hisseler* (Religious Stories and Their Morals), p. 233.

of Supreme Gathering) before the Sirat bridge, in darkness."

The man then asked, "Who will be among those to cross the bridge first?" and the Prophet answered, "Those who abandoned their homelands and migrated for the sake of Allah."[72]

72 Muslim, Hayd, 34.

Heaven and Hell

Advancing towards Paradise

On that Day, you will see the believing men and the believing women (led swiftly toward Paradise), with their light shining forth before them and on their right hands. "Glad tidings for you today: Gardens through which rivers flow, (into which you will enter) to abide therein! This is indeed the supreme triumph." On that Day, the hypocritical men and the hypocritical women will say to those who believe: "Wait for us, that we may have some light from your light." It will be said: "Turn back (if you can, to the world where such light was to be obtained), and seek light (through your deeds you did there)." Just then a wall of separation will be put between them, with a gate therein (through which the hypocrites, so as to increase their regret, will observe the state of the believers). The inner side of the wall (which will separate the believers from the hypocrites) – there will be in it the mercy (of eternal happiness), and outside it there will be the punishment (of eternal doom). (Al-Hadid 57:12–13)[73]

---

[73] As understood from the Qur'anic verses above, the believers will advance toward Paradise on the right side *"with their light shining forth before them and on their right hands,"* while the hypocrites, who are truly unbelievers and will thus receive their records of deeds in their left hands, will advance toward Hell on the left side, and be left behind because of being enveloped by the darkness produced by their unbelief, hypocrisy, and evil deeds. (See Ünal, 2008, p.

They Are Not Equal

Is he who is a believer like him who is a transgressor? They are not equal. As for those who believe and do good, righteous deeds, for them are Gardens of Refuge and Dwelling, as a welcome (from Allah, in return) for what they have been doing. But as for those who transgress (the bounds set by Allah in belief and action), their refuge and dwelling is the Fire. Every time they desire to come out of it, they will be returned to it, and they will be told, "Taste the punishment of the Fire which you used to deny." (As-Sajdah 32:18–20)

The Fact of the Matter

Hanzala al-Usayyid, one of the scribes of the Messenger of Allah, reported: "One day, the Messenger of Allah told us about Heaven and Hell; he described them to such an extent that it was as if we were observing them with our own eyes. Then I departed and returned home to my family, where we laughed and had fun.

At that time suddenly I was reminded of the spirituality I had felt when in the company of the Messenger of

---

1109). The light of the believers is to be sent forth from the world through their good, righteous deeds. The more deeds there are and the more sincerely they are done, the greater and brighter is the light that they will produce. (Ed.)

Allah. Immediately I ran outside and began to weep. Abu Bakr, who was passing by at the time, asked, 'Hanzala! What is wrong?' I replied, 'O Abu Bakr! I am a hypocrite.'

Abu Bakr then asked, 'But why?' So I explained, 'When I am in the company of the Messenger of Allah, he continuously reminds us of Heaven and Hell. It is as if we are actually seeing them with our own eyes. But when we leave his company, we continue our daily lives, laughing and talking with our families, and we forget most of what he has taught us.' Abu Bakr said, 'I swear by Allah, I have experienced the same thing.'"

So together, they went to the Prophet and explained their concerns, and the Prophet replied, "I swear by Allah! If your spirituality continued at the same level as you were in my presence, the angels would come and shake hands with you, and they would be with you wherever you go. But Hanzala! The fact of the matter is that you should devote some of your time to worshipping Allah and some of your time to your worldly affairs. But you should never forget your Lord while you are engaged in worldly affairs!"[74]

---

[74] Muslim, Tawbah, 12–13; Tirmidhi, Qiyamah, 59; Musnad Ahmad, Vol. 4, p. 346.

The Gates of Paradise

Our beloved Prophet said, "On the Day of Judgment, I will go to the gates of Paradise and ask for them to be opened. Khâzin, the guardian angel of the gates of Paradise, will ask, 'Who are you?' I will reply, 'I am Muhammad.'

Then the angel will say, 'I was ordered not to open the gates for anyone before. But I am opening the gates for you.'"[75]

Chambers, Mansions and Palaces

"The inhabitants of the chambers of Paradise are those who speak in a gentle manner, continuously fast, and pray at night while others are sleeping.[76] A mansion of Paradise will be built for those who build a mosque for the sake of Allah.[77] Allah will grant a mansion in Paradise for those who (regularly) perform four units before and two units after (the *fard* of) the Noon Prayer, two units after (the *fard* of) the Evening Prayer, two units after (the *fard* of) the Night Prayer, and two units before (the

---

[75]   Muslim, Iman, 333.

[76]   Tirmidhi, Birr, 53.

[77]   Nasai, Masjid, 1.

fard of) the Morning Prayer, making twelve-units of (the Sunnah) Prayers in total.[78] Those who bear patiently the death of their child will be given a palace in Paradise.[79] Those who refrain from disputing even if they are in the right, those who abandon lying, even if it is in jest, and those whose manners are honorable will be given a palace in the center of Paradise.[80] Whoever visits the sick will be rewarded with a mansion and garden in Paradise."[81]

The Trees of Paradise

Describing the trees of Paradise, our beloved Prophet said, "There is a tree in Paradise under which a person on a mount can travel for a hundred years, but not be able to cover the distance spanned by its shade.[82] In the center of Paradise is an amazing tree, its shade spans across the dwellings of the distinguished residents. Every branch bears the names of the habitants of Paradise. It produces every kind of fruit you could imagine. The groomed, saddled horses and reined camels are also pre-

---

[78] Tirmidhi, Salah, 206; Nasai, Qiyamu'l-Layl, 66; Ibn Majah, Iqamah, 100.

[79] Tirmidhi, Janaiz, 36.

[80] Abu Dawud, Adab, 7.

[81] Tirmidhi, Birr, 64; Abu Dawud, Janaiz, 7; Ibn Majah, Janaiz, 2.

[82] Tirmidhi, Tafsir (al-Waqi'ah), 57, Jannah, 1.

pared. This tree with a golden trunk spreads a scent that covers a distance of forty, seventy, a hundred, five hundred, or even a thousand years.[83] There is not a tree in Paradise that does not have a trunk made of gold."[84]

Asking for Paradise

One day our beloved Prophet was asked, "What is Paradise?" He replied, "Paradise is the place of eternal abode, shining light, lingering fragrance, a well-established, lofty palace, a flowing stream, a place of ripe fruit, greenery, joy and, refreshment.[85] Its bricks are of silver and gold, its mortar is of fragrant musk, its pebbles are of pearl and sapphire, and its soil is saffron.[86] Paradise has one hundred levels, and the distance between every level is as vast as the distance between the heavens and the earth. The highest is the Gardens of al-Firdaws,[87] and from it originates the four rivers of Paradise. Above the Gardens

---

83 Musnad Ahmad, Vol. 4, p. 237; Vol. 5, pp. 27, 46, 50–51.

84 Tirmidhi, Jannah, 1.

85 Ibn Majah, Jannah, 39.

86 Tirmidhi, Jannah, 2.

87 As it is revealed in the Qur'an, "*Allah has promised the believers, both men and women, Gardens through which rivers flow, therein to abide, and blessed dwellings in Gardens of perpetual bliss (Jannatu 'Adn); and greater (than those) is Allah's being pleased with them. That indeed is the supreme triumph.*" (At-Tawbah 9:72)

of al-Firdaws is the Divine Throne. So when you ask of the gardens of Paradise from your Lord, ask for the gardens of al-Firdaws, the highest level of Paradise."[88]

Indeed, both the Qur'an and the Practice of the Prophet attach a great importance to attaining the Divine pleasure. As there is nothing better than the Divine pleasure, nothing exceeds the attainment of Allah's good pleasure. Therefore, looking for paths on how to attain the pleasure of Allah is such a valuable thing in the sight of a believer that all other things appear to be less important in comparison. In fact, the attainment of Allah's good pleasure is even better than the dwellings, maidens, delicious food, fruits and drinks, or any other physical pleasures of the Gardens of perpetual bliss (Jannatu 'Adn).

Allah the Almighty loves and befriends some of His servants who strive for His cause and ask Him for His pleasure and friendship, further blessing them in the Hereafter with the Gardens of al-Firdaws (Jannatu'l-Firdaws)—the highest abode or level of Paradise. The Firdaws signifies, therefore, Allah's greater or particular good pleasure, or His being more pleased with these servants of Him. Actually, Allah will be pleased with all the people of Paradise, but "Allah's greater or particular good pleasure" is the greatest of the bounties of Paradise, one so profound and exceptional that one favored with it no longer needs another bounty and pleasure. (See also Gülen, Reflections on the Qur'an, 2012, pp. 129–130).

It is because of this superiority of the Gardens of al-Firdaws over other abodes or levels of Paradise that our beloved Prophet advised his community to ask for al-Firdaws. As understood from the relevant hadiths, the Gardens of Firdaws is such a superior place in Paradise that those who dwell there will be able to observe all the layers of Paradise. (Ed.)

[88] Tirmidhi, Jannah, 4.

Like Brilliant Stars

One day the Messenger of Allah explained how the people dwelling in lofty chambers in the higher levels of Paradise will be seen by those below them as if one were looking at a brilliant star shining far away on the horizon: "The people of Paradise will look at the people dwelling in the chambers above them in the same way you look at the stars moving from the east to the west on the horizon like shining pearls. Their difference in virtue (and thus in rank) will show the ones dwelling in the chambers so high above them."

Upon this the Companions asked, "O Messenger of Allah! Are these the dwellings of the Prophets; are they the stations or abodes that nobody else can reach?" The Prophet replied, "No! I swear by the One Who holds my life in the power of His hand! The inhabitants of these chambers are not the Prophets, but rather the ones who believe in Allah and confirm His Prophets."[89]

Accompany You in Paradise

Ibn Ka'b al-Aslami reported, "I accompanied the Messenger of Allah one night. I gave him water to perform his ablutions and helped him. He told me, 'Is there any-

---

89 Bukhari, Bad'ul-Khalq, 8; Muslim, Jannah, 11.

thing you ask of me?' 'I wish to accompany you in Paradise,' I replied.

Upon this he asked, 'Or maybe something else other than this?' So I answered, 'No, I want nothing but this, O Messenger of Allah.' He then said, 'Then help me by devoting yourself to much prostration in worship.'"[90]

The Breath of Hell

Prophet Muhammad, peace and blessings be upon him, said, "Hell complained to its Lord, saying: 'O Lord! My parts are eating up (destroying) one another!' So Allah permitted Hell to take two breaths (so as not to eat itself away), one in the winter, which is why you feel severe cold, and one in the summer, which is why you feel the severe heat."[91]

The River of Paradise

Regarding those who will not be able to drink from the Kawthar (river of Paradise), the Messenger of Allah said, "I will arrive at the Kawthar before you.

---

90   Muslim, Salah, 226; Abu Dawud, Salah, 312.
91   Bukhari, Mawaqit, 8, Bad'ul-Khalq, 10; Muslim, Masjid, 185.

Some of you will be shown to me to such an extent that if I lean over I will touch them, but they will pull back. I will say, 'O Lord! They are my followers!'

Then I will be told, 'You are unaware of how they innovated in the religion after you.' So I will say, 'May those who have (invented innovations, and thereby) changed the religion after me be distant from Your Mercy.'"[92]

Patience at the Time of Grief

A woman came to the beloved Prophet and said, "O Messenger of Allah! Pray that I may go to Paradise, for I have lost three children."

The Prophet listened to the woman's words of grief and said, "You have already prepared your place in Paradise."[93]

A Mansion in Paradise

Bahlul Dana, one of the saints of the period of Caliph Harun Rashid, was constructing something from smoothly trimmed planks of wood, something that

---

92 Bukhari, Riqaq, 53, 1; Muslim, Fadail, 32.
93 Bukhari, Jannah, 45; Abu Dawud, Iman, 45.

resembled a house. When Zubayda, Harun Rashid's wife, inquired as to what he was building, he replied, "A mansion in Paradise."

Zubayda, a very religious woman, asked him, "Can I buy this mansion?" Bahlul Dana replied, "If you really want it, I will sell it to you." Then she asked, "How much will you sell it for?" He answered, "One silver coin."

So without hesitation, the caliph's wife agreed and gave Bahlul Dana a silver coin. That night, both Harun Rashid and his wife had a dream in which they were in Paradise: Zubayda was sitting in her grand mansion, and Harun Rashid came and asked her, "When did you get this mansion my dear?" She replied, "I brought it from Bahlul yesterday for one silver coin."

Early the next morning, the caliph asked his servant to call Bahlul. When he arrived, Harun Rashid asked Bahlul without telling him about his dream: "Can you build me a mansion identical to the one you sold my wife yesterday?" Bahlul replied, "Yes, of course I can." So the Caliph asked, "How much do you want for it?" "A thousand silver coins," replied Bahlul.

The caliph, looking totally surprised, said, "But you sold it to my wife for one silver coin." So Bahlul replied, "Yes I sold it to your wife for a silver coin, but she bought the mansion with no knowledge of its true value, whereas you saw how magnificent the mansion was last night (in your dream). Therefore, I think you should pay accordingly."[94]

A Shield against the Flames of Hell

Aisha, the dear wife of the Prophet, said, "One day a woman came with her two daughters and asked me for help. At the time I had nothing to give them but a single date. So I gave her the date, and she took it and divided the date into two, then without eating any herself, she gave both of her daughters an equal share of the date.

I was deeply touched, and when I told the Messenger of Allah he stated (as follows):

'Whoever treats their daughters with kindness, they will intercede for them on the Day of Judgment. Whoever raises two daughters until they reach maturity, we will be (so close) like this on the Day of Judgment (joining together his two fingers).

Whoever raises three daughters or sisters, or two daughters or sisters, and treats them with love and kindness, and gives them in marriage when they reach a suitable age,

---

94 *Evliyalar Ansiklopedisi* (Encyclopedia of the Saints), see the entry for Bahlul Dana, Istanbul: Türkiye Gazetesi, p. 45.

they will be rewarded with Paradise. Whoever has two daughters and treats them fairly and does not prefer their sons over them will be granted Paradise."[95]

When Parents Reach Old Age

The Prophet repeated three times, "May he be disgraced, may he be disgraced, may he be disgraced!"

So the Companions asked, "O Messenger of Allah! Who?" The Prophet replied, "The person who sees their parents reach old age, either one or both of them, but does not enter Paradise (by taking care of and treating them well)."[96]

Do You Have a Mother?

One day a youth named Jahimah came to the Prophet and said, "O Messenger of Allah! I also want to fight for the cause of Allah, and I have come to ask your advice."

---

[95] Bukhari, Zakah, 10, Adab, 19; Muslim, Birr, 147; Tirmidhi, Birr, 13; Abu Dawud, Adab, 130.

[96] Muslim, Birr, 9; Tirmidhi, Da'awat, 110.

The Prophet asked him, "Do you have a mother?" He replied, "Yes." Then the Prophet said, "Remain with your mother (and take care of her as your striving for the cause of Allah), for Paradise lies beneath her feet."[97]

When the Prophet said, "Paradise lies beneath the feet of mothers," he was asked, "What are the rights of fathers?" He replied, "The pleasure of a father lies in the pleasure of Allah, and his displeasure lies in the displeasure of Allah."[98]

Opening and Closing the Gates

One day, following the death of the dear Prophet, Uthman was sitting outside his home. Umar passed by and greeted him, but Uthman did not return his greetings. So Umar went to Abu Bakr and explained what had happened. Hearing this, Abu Bakr said, "O Umar! Be patient, he may have had a good excuse for not returning your greetings."

Caliph Abu Bakr then sent his servant to summon Uthman. When he arrived, Abu Bakr asked him, "O Uthman! You know how the Prophet valued and honored Umar, so why did you not return his greetings?" Uthman

---

97 Nasai, Jihad, 5.
98 Tirmidhi, Birr, 3.

replied, "O Caliph of the Messenger of Allah! I did not hear him, for at the time I was in a state of sorrow and grief." So Abu Bakr asked, "What grieved you to such an extent that you were unable accept his greetings?"

Uthman explained, "I was sitting there contemplating that although I had spent so much time in the company of Allah's Messenger, never once did I ask him which words close the gates to Hell, and which words open the gates to Paradise." Abu Bakr replied, "O Uthman! You truly have a valid excuse for not returning Umar's greetings, forgive me (for asking). Rest assured, I have glad tidings to give you. I once asked the Prophet, 'O Messenger of Allah! How can we close the gates of Hell, and open the gates of Paradise?' He replied, 'With the testimony of faith I offered to my uncle Abu Talib (as there is nothing which outweighs embracing the true faith).'"[99]

---

[99] M. Yusuf Kandahlawi, *Hayatu's Sahabah* (Trans.), Semerkand Publishers.

The Generous
in Heaven

The Eight Gateways
into Paradise

Describing the gates of Paradise our beloved Prophet said, "On the first gate is the inscription: '*Lâ ilâha illa'llâh Muhammadun Rasûlullah*' (There is no deity but Allah, and Muhammad is His Messenger), this is the gate for the Prophets, the martyrs, and the generous.

"The second gate is for those who perform the ablution free of defect and establish the Prayer in perfect conformity with its conditions. The third is the gate of those who give in the prescribed purifying alms. The fourth is for those who enjoin and promote what is right and good and forbid and try to prevent evil. The fifth is the gate for those who observe fasting. The sixth is the gate of those who perform the major and minor pilgrimages. The seventh is the gate for those who strive for Islam. The eighth is the gate for the pious and for those who lower their gaze from that which is forbidden in religion.

"The guardian angels of the gates of Paradise will surely welcome the believing servant who spends one of the two things from his wealth for the cause of Allah, and each and every one of them will invite him to enter Paradise through the very gate they guard."[100]

Spending for Divine Pleasure

As for him who gives (out of his wealth for the pleasure of Allah), and keeps from disobedience to Him in reverence for Him and piety, and affirms the best (in creed, action, and the reward to be given), We will make easy for him the path to the state of ease (salvation after an easy reckoning). But as for him who is niggardly and regards himself as self-sufficient in independence of Him, and denies the best (in creed, action, and the reward to be given), We will make easy for him the path to hardship (punishment after a hard reckoning). And his wealth will not avail him when he falls to ruin. (Al-Layl 92:5–11)

The Night of the Ascension

The Messenger of Allah told his Companions, "On the night of the Ascension, I saw an inscription on the gates of Paradise: 'Charity will be rewarded ten times,

---

[100] Nasai, Jihad, 45.

and loans (will be rewarded) eighteen times.' So I asked Gabriel, 'O Gabriel! Why is something given as a loan superior to charitable giving?' He replied, 'Even if he has money, a beggar (on most occasions) will beg for charity. Whereas a man who asks for a loan is asking because he is in need.'"[101]

While Your Neighbor Is Hungry

Abu Dharr, one of the Companions of the blessed Messenger, was explaining that a Muslim should not sleep while they are full when their neighbor is hungry. He warned the people that those who live a life of prosperity while their Muslim brothers are in a state of poverty or struggling in debt would be subjected to the harsh punishment of Hell. So to judge his sincerity, the people sent him a pouch full of gold coins and asked him to accept it as a gift.

When Abu Dharr refused, telling the servant who had brought him the money to give it to those less fortunate than himself, the servant replied, "They told me that if you accept the money, I will be freed." Hearing this, Abu Dharr had no choice but to accept the money.

---

[101] Ibrahim Canan, *Hadis Ansiklopedisi* (Encyclopedia of Hadith), Vol. 17, p. 300.

The next morning, the servant returned and said, "The money I gave you was for somebody else, I gave it to you by mistake. Can you return it to me?"

Abu Dharr replied, "There was no way that I could have kept that money and lived in prosperity while my neighbors were hungry and struggling in poverty. So I shared it between the poor as soon as you left, therefore I have no money to give you."[102]

Even Half a Date

Aisha, the beloved wife of the Prophet, hired a servant to help her with the house chores. But Archangel Gabriel came to the Prophet before the servant had the opportunity to reach home and said, "Send the servant away from you and your family, she is destined for Hell." So they did, and Aisha gave her some dates to eat on the journey.

On her way back, the servant came across someone who was obviously very poor. She felt so sorry for this person that she gave him half of her dates; the hungry man was very grateful for her kindness.

---

[102] Ahmet Şahin, *Aradığımız İslam* (The Islam We Seek), pp. 68–69.

Then Archangel Gabriel returned to the Prophet and said, "O Muhammad! Allah has given you permission to call the servant back." When the Prophet inquired as to the reason, Gabriel said, "She gave half of her dates to a poor person for the sake of Allah, this is why Allah forgave her and saved her from the destruction of Hell."

The Prophet later told his Companions, "Save yourselves from the Hellfire, even if it is giving half a date in charity."[103]/[104]

Giving Charity for the Dead

A man came to the Prophet and asked, "O Messenger of Allah! My mother died suddenly before she had the opportunity to make a will. If I give charity on her behalf, will this be written as a good, righteous deed for her?" The Prophet answered, "Yes it will."[105]

---

[103] A good deed, however small it is, may attract the Divine forgiveness and save one from Hellfire. Indeed, a minute sincere act can be granted an enormous reward that one can never imagine and may weigh heavier than masses of insincere deeds.

[104] Bukhari, Birr, 35.

[105] Bukhari, Janaiz, 94; Muslim, Zakah, 15; Musnad Ahmad, Vol. 2, p. 371.

Caring for an Orphan

Joining his middle and index fingers, our beloved Prophet said, "I will be like this with the guardian of an orphan in Paradise.[106] Whoever takes an orphan from among the Muslims and feeds him or her, as long as they have not committed the unforgivable sin (of associating partners with Allah), Allah will surely grant them Paradise."[107]

---

[106] Bukhari, Talaq, 14; Adab, 24; Tirmidhi, Birr, 14; Abu Dawud, Adab, 131.

[107] Tirmidhi, Birr, 14.

Intercession

Those Who Die without Associating Partners with Allah

"Every Messenger has a supplication that will be accepted by Allah, and all the Prophets employed haste in making this supplication. I have saved my supplication as an intercession for my followers on the Day of Judgment. This supplication will be for those of my followers who die without associating partners with Allah."[108]

I Will Intercede

Prophet Muhammad, peace and blessings be upon him, went to visit his uncle Abu Talib on his death bed. Abu Jahl was among the few disbelievers who were also sitting in the room with Abu Talib. The Prophet said,

108 Bukhari, Da'awat, 1, Tawhid, 31; Muslim, Iman, 334, (198); Muwatta, Qur'an 26, (1, 212); Tirmidhi, Da'awat, 141, (3597).

"Uncle! Recite the words '*Lâ ilâha illa'llah*' (There is no deity but Allah) and I will intercede for you in the presence of Allah." Then Abu Jahl turned to Abu Talib and intervened, "Are you really going to abandon the religion of Abdulmuttalib (i.e., the polytheist religion of your forefathers)?"

In the hope that he would embrace Islam, the Prophet continued to recite the testimony of faith to his uncle. But the disbelievers persisted in their intervention, and consistently repeated their words. Then Abu Talib declared, "I will continue to follow the old religion of Abdulmuttalib!"

Abu Talib refused to recite the testimony of faith, so with a deep sense of sorrow the Prophet said, "I will continue to ask Allah for your forgiveness, until I am forbidden to do so." Then the following verses of the Qur'an were revealed:

> *It is not (fitting) for the Prophet and those who believe to ask Allah for the forgiveness of those who associate partners with Allah, even though they be near of kin, after it has become clear to them that they (died polytheists and, therefore,) are condemned to the Blazing Flame.* (At-Tawbah 9:113)

> *You cannot guide to truth whomever you like, but Allah guides whomever He wills. He knows best who are guided (and amenable to guidance).* (Al-Qasas 28:56)[109]

---

[109] Bukhari, Ansar, 40, Janaiz, 81, Qasas, 1, Iman, 19; Muslim, Iman, 39.

After Death

"Among the good, righteous deeds that continue to benefit a believer after death are knowledge that they have taught and conveyed to others, the righteous child who lives after them, the Book of the Qur'an that they have copied and left as legacy, a mosque that they have had built, a house that they have built for wayfarers, and charity that they have given from their wealth while alive (so that they may be rewarded after death.)"[110]

The Prayer of a Child

Prophet Muhammad, peace and blessings be upon him, said, "Allah the Almighty will raise the rank of a righteous servant in Paradise. And then he will ask, 'O Lord! How did this intercession for lofty rank happen?' And Allah will reply, 'Your child prayed for your forgiveness (following your death).'"[111]

---

110 Ibn Majah, Muqaddamah, 20.
111 Ibn Majah, Adab, 1; Musnad Ahmad, Vol. 2, p. 509.

The Intercession of
a Deceased Child

The female Companions went to the Prophet and said, "O Messenger of Allah! In regards to learning the religion, men are more fortunate than us. Can you dedicate a day for the women; we too want to learn about the religion from you."

So the Prophet arranged a day for the women; during the sermon he talked to them about many subjects, saying: "Whoever among you has lost three children, they will certainly intercede for you against (and you will thus be screened from) the Flames of Hell."

One of the women then asked, "O Messenger of Allah! What if she has lost two?" The Prophet replied, "Even if she has lost two.[112] If a person loses their beloved child and bears the grief with patience, seeking reward, Allah will not be pleased with any other reward for them but to grant them Paradise."[113]

---

[112] Musnad Ahmad, Vol. 1, p. 363.
[113] Tirmidhi, Zuhd, 58, Janaiz, 36; Nasai, Janaiz, 23.

The Intercession of the Memorizers of the Qur'an

Explaining the importance and virtues of memorizing the Qur'an, our beloved Prophet said, "On the Day of Judgment, a crown will be placed on the heads of the parents whose child reads the Qur'an and abides by its commands. The light of this crown will be brighter than the light of the sun even if the sun itself was within their home. Thus, can you imagine the light of the one who recites the Qur'an themselves and acts upon its commands?"[114]

"Whoever recites and memorizes the Qur'an and accepts that which is deemed as lawful in the Qur'an as lawful and that which is unlawful in the Book as unlawful, Allah will grant him Paradise. And Allah will accept his intercession for ten members of his family entering Hell, and they will also be admitted into Paradise."[115]

---

[114] Abu Dawud, Salah, 349.

[115] Tirmidhi, Sawabu'l-Qur'an, 13; Muhittin Akgul, *Kur'an Okumanın Önemi* (The Importance of Reading and Reciting the Qur'an), p. 72.